FEELER

HEATHER McHUGH

Quarternote Chapbook Series #17

T0098974

Sarabande Books
Louisville, KY

FIRST EDITION
All rights reserved.
No part of this book may be reproduced without written permission of the
publisher.

Library of Congress Cataloging-in-Publication Data

Names: McHugh, Heather, 1948- author.
Title: Feeler / poems by Heather McHugh.
Description: First edition. | Louisville, KY : Sarabande Books, [2019] |
Series: Quarternote chapbook series
Identifiers: LCCN 2019006378 (print) | LCCN 2019009646 (ebook) | ISBN
9781946448439 (ebook) | ISBN 9781946448422 (pbk. : alk. paper)
Classification: LCC PS3563.A311614 (ebook) | LCC PS3563.A311614 A6 2019
(print) | DDC 811/.54--dc23
LC record available at https://lccn.loc.gov/2019006378

Interior and exterior design by Danika Isdahl.
Cover image is a public domain image by Karen Perez produced as part of the Insects
Unlocked project at The University of Texas at Austin.

Manufactured in Canada.
This book is printed on acid-free paper.
Sarabande Books is a nonprofit literary organization.

This project is supported in part by an award from the National Endowment for the
Arts. The Kentucky Arts Council, the state arts agency, supports Sarabande Books
with state tax dollars and federal funding from the National
Endowment for the Arts.

For Ellen Bryant Voigt
(one tough mama)

Contents

FEELER

For the Record

Compelled for all those years
to record what I saw,
what I felt, what I thought—
in all precision and intensity—

Did I have too much time? I think not.
Or I feel not.

Nowadays I cannot tell
the two apart: can't feel things thoughtlessly
or think things up without emotion. The world felt
endless to me then, perhaps, and needing
categories, angles, clear containers.
Stillest shots and lyric seizures, insights built
on glances, glimpses.
Later, glosses were applied.

But then the vitreous
detaches, first in one eye then
a few weeks later in the other
(flashes from a corner of your vision
settle into shorter threads
that float first one way then

another, as if down
the slip-curve of the globe). Forever
after that, the world is slightly blurred, it's
mediated, it is not immediate.
And as for thought, well,
thought is not

the curve, and not
the gloss, and not the thread

or snippet, certainly it isn't any
thought-luster behind the scenes,
inside the seeing, bothered by the
intervening gauze, but eager
to ignite another seer. No, no,
the thought can be
forgiven as
foregone:

it does its best, and
loves its things.
But things were never clear.

The Missing Glove

I

A glance is a blow—
a force you feel,
or feel he feels, the more
your car obtrudes into

his lit proximity: the one
arms-length of curb between
these traffic cataracts
contrarily aflow, now
slowing to a crawl, and then
to a pause of purring steel,
to bring the likes of you

eventually face to face
with the likes
of him.

II

Perhaps you fear
that forwardness of his,
and that unarmored gaze, his own
near-ominous
near-odious
near intimacy.

III

With a touch, you make
your door secure—
an all-but-in-

offensive click.
What now, with such
a naked stretch of red light

set against us? Set about
your pantomime—the one
in which you cannot find,

at length, in the
glove compartment,
something you are missing.

IV

Needless to say there hasn't
been a glove in there
since nineteen thirty-five—

you can be sure
the light will change before
a fucking glove appears. A shrug

might work. ("We only
came out for a ride!") Or how
about a sing-along? (To tell the fella

that we care: "We will not stay,
we will not stare. We wish to spare
the ones who plead. We know that you

would rather never
be regarded
in such need.")

V

Look up, and you see red.
Look left and you behold
him holding up his sign.

Look right, so no one
notices the way
he touched your fender, turned your head . . .

VI

You turn your head and then you find
the feeling's everywhere. It's in the guilty-
looking truck, it's in the passing of the passerby,
it woos a woman from her break, unmans mechanics
at the shop, besets the tourists on their rounds, and snares
the sonneteer. No matter what we do, the world

is where we're stuck. For shame or mercy,
dark or bright, it means to find
a way inside. You've closed
your mind, you can't do more:

You can't get out of sight.

From Sea to Sea

For Dot and Harlan Gardner

1. A Bay Is a Sound

The fish have subtler schools
Than ours, and do not read

The do-not-enter signs.
The strictest cedar stands on no

"My-air-your-water" legal grounds
(Though we have fed our toxins

Through the tree, whose systems
So resemble those

Of human nerve: We bleed and we
Feel blent). No matter from

What quarries into air the marks
Of capitals and shares and pseudo-

Independences be piled
(To keep some people

Reassured, and some reviled)
There still is born

This moving character, whose chairs
Are wheeled, whose tablets

(Cellular and pharmaceutical) are not
Addiction to, but dictionary of,

Our flair for connectivity. We grew
To care for nature; she is nature's

Child, our wild
Reheartening, reminder of

Our luckiest identity. (As what?
As citizens of everywhere.)

2. Humptulips Once Loved Meddybemps

Then Meddybemps became
A clean-up site. The past appeals
Until it just appalls; the trail
A way, a cause, until the curse
Recurs. Port Gamble's still

A little tinglish
From the rained-on
Revved-up powersaws.
Its evergreening history's adored
As fiercely as Machias's.

A few of us continue pinging
Forthwest and anon
On our arcane affinities.
No quirks of archaism cramp
The busted meter of the limpet's style;
The whales wail sensitively
At the amplitudes.

Only a local rag at first (its content
Lumberjacketed, disdained by droves
Of citybro on break) would air the latest news
Of border weapons tests (wave-frequencies), in case
Someone was listening. (The capitals are deafened
By securitizing prose. The ledger's tilted
Sharply on the ledge. It gives a fart
About the tender
in the endless sway.)
One hardly knows

The cautionary from conclusive, among signs,
As now (from sea to sea, first fiercely, then afar)

The starfish feel their feelers melt away.

Bad Dream for Life

Gleaming plazas kept all seven
edifices constantly attuned
to Commerce Central, each façade
untouched by any

shadow of a doubt. Through several
overbearing portals, high and low, on urgent errands
(with a super-subtle humming and a calm dispatch)
some six or seven state-of-the-art smart

Personal Flying Devices kept on
minding everybody's business. Under the drone
of cool efficiencies, among the statues in the square, I was
a mess, the only human there, the only one without

a PFD, without a ghosted chance.
Dull-footed, lacking glitterwork, I darted
here and there, from dark to dark. (So far
the statues shed more shade

than glances. They'd be the very last
of the throw-back arts.) The most prestigious of
the government departments was the ICU,
where Interspecies Clean-Up was both

headquartered and motherboarded. (Friends
had wandered there, in hopes of mercy, if not of repair. I'd no
such dreams.) The hazard of my presence, in its stark peculiarity,
remained, till now, entirely unremarked. The worker bees

were only temporarily distracted, as assembly lines
poured forth the Immortalities, all finally designed.
I was unfixable, and feverish, and fat, a splotch
of Generation H, but I was still

beneath the notice of the zoomers.
(Twenty-six is nowhere near enough.) It all
was a matter of time. And heaven knows what
hardware, in what passes for a mind,

was keeping that.

To Be Expected

How generous can comprehending be?
Is all of it the outgrowth of a baby's
grip? (What mothers suffer from, and then

without.) If health is change,
and if the healthy give
their seizures up, why can't I let

my own attachments pass? I've felt
four times the awesome, awful
clawing from the bed

of mortal matter's state: Two friends,
two ancestors. Each one upon the deathbed
held so fast the holding actually hurt

my hand. Yet it was love. And never
from a healthy soul have I encountered
grips so unrelenting. All they wanted

was for both of us to stay.
I slipped away, so they did too.
And when it was my need

to say of love, for love, and to my living love,
how terrible those grasps had been,
how unexpected were the sheer

uncanny final strengths
the dying had, how literal their grip
on life, he (ever-undemonstrative) replied:

That's a cliché.

Everybody Has a Fatal Disease

*

In the night, while it's quiet, I run
some lips across its ribs, some eyeteeth over
knucklebones, some mind downspine.

*

The saddest dog alive could still feel love. If you must feel
a feeling, that one's
fine. And if you want, there's this

refinement: feeling in
the transitive.

*

To comfort one another,
not to smother.

*

Once love
is feelable, a want
is born. Kind of

comparative. (Comparative
of kind.) The kinder
come in time to be

indicative. (Forget
superlative, that
cloying fiction: It's the index

we are always
losing touches with,
and putting touches on.)

*

Life's one condition:
being its own
precondition.

Yet as far as
mind can tell, no time's
repeatable.

*

May I take
pictures of

your poor
afflicted pelt?

I am a well-meaning
American.

*

Life/death:
are you insured?

It's mutual.

From what is hard
to parse, or to control, or be
unimplicated by,

instinctively the lookers
turn their eyes. (The blind man
has more sense.)

*

The terror in the mirror: it suggests
a gaze. The first gaze ever met was made
a double present of, and so became
an obstacle
to vision.

*

Absurd!
You hear?

*

One feels for
one's own self, but art

feels for another.
Smothered, we're

disposed to smother,
then become ourselves

re-smotherable once again.
So life's a mother.

(Of predicaments it is
the father, too. The DNA of the
indictment. Every creature choked
with feeling.) Life! The uncommuted
sentence.

*

Look here. Look right smack
here, or else

I cannot read your lips.

Shots in the ICU

The unwritten CDs have stripes
of spectrum down their faces, there in their
transparent cases—perfect traces of
what otherwise were mere
idea or metaphor . . . some gist
or twist or history
of light. The pure

appearance of
refraction in these lines
can shift into the vertical;
it's utterly resistant to
the daily laterals and dull
collaterals; its otherworldliness
is wildest for precision: close-up rainbow
several millimeters wide, a dwelling place
for uncontainables (in analytic radiance) to run
from the outer edge of a disc straight toward
its center, not in coils, concentric (as upon his old LPs),
but deepening in radii from
two to three toward four

dimensions. His bifocals taken
from him and his hopes extinguished, Dad
keeps hissing life's a swindle. Birthing room
to deathbed, that's the line—a legacy from
sunlight, long profession now inclined
to sharpness, as the read-outs turn
to shout-outs, shivers from Intensive Care's own
backed-up window-ledge. I got the gene
for breaking, and for vertical evasions. Rest my sights
upon the plumb-line

down the centers of
the stacked CDs. Unreadable
they were, and blessedly, until
a setting star brings back
the comedy in it for me,
and rods and cones
inform the living hole again with all
those spikes of spindly evidence. O lazy
pupil! Crazy cornucopia! For I was blind,

and you were blind, but now we have myopia.

Shape Up, Says Doctor Death
Thanks to NBP, and after Blaga Dimitrova

Who's sicker? Someone saying
Just the one thing, over and over,
Or the one who runs
From repetition, as from conscience?

The man who lost himself—is he
The most afflicted? Or the man who's always
Seeking second selves,
The realer ones?

Can't you recall your name?
Or do you go around
Reminding people of it?
Which is sicker? Come on, now,

Red-blooded health—
Let's take a breath,
Let's fill that chest!
What's this

Small chime I'm hearing
Near the ticker?—bit of broken
Nerve? A spot of bad self-pity? Bloody
Wheezing in the deep? Enough of

That! It's time to study
What the dying do:
Sobbing to laugh.
Singing to weep.

Wandering at Night

God, a dog,
they say, big deal,
get over it, OK?
"Worse than a dog" is how
my drunken mother said my father,
all but dead in the hospice ward where she
knew better than to visit him, was being treated
by his kids (though all she knew of it was my
report each night before I crashed in the hotel.
That night I'd said we'd like her help
with the obituary).

Really what she meant was
she felt like a dog herself—
he'd dumped her once upon a time and then,
when Wife the Second died, he came again
to ask her hand. As she was nine years younger, she
could see what that entailed. With righteous
indignation she said no.

And really what she meant was she
was terribly afraid of her own death, and his;
afraid as well that she'd become (in her
imagination of our own imaginations)
something to neglect. In fact
was sad for him, and for herself
who'd wound up left-out, riddled
through and through with guilt,
unconsciously unkind.

I loved the dog beyond—
as sensible accounts would say—
all reason. Poured into the vessel of

his patient, bestial regard my sediments
of sentiment, my heaviness of love.
His belly hung its weighted hammock
from the tentpoles of his hips; he groaned
when he lay down; and after two long seizures,
when he most required to sleep, we mercifully
arranged for him to die. We cannot seem
to love ourselves as much. The course of aging's

clearly not a cruise, a friendly sky,
a warmer toddy: it's a grind. Until it dies,
a body loses sleep. It's born to lose
the everything-in-mind

it meant to keep.

The Truly Screaming Baby

Thank god says the woman in 13E
we're not back there. She means
back there with the mom
with the truly screaming baby
and the two toddlers more to boot
who didn't once (my seatmate
sourly now informs me)
in the pre-board waiting area obey
a word she said. The baby sounds
in agony. We haven't even yet entirely
taxi'd out to take-off. Not a passenger
appears remotely sympathetic, and I can't

help wincing on the mom's behalf.
What if the baby's sick what if
she's always like this and the mother's feeling
permanently miserable since even on this
getaway she cannot get away
what is a flight if not an escapade and now
her fellow passengers are blaming her
for what she can't escape or even partially
ameliorate what if they're penniless and this
is her one chance to visit relatives what if the father's
always off carousing and comes home for just
an hour or two at most to get her pregnant once again
then take her just as much to task for noise
as these more pampered people
on the airplane do and what
could make a baby's life so utterly
unbearable who has no words
to say it better here for us it's
just a hundred twenty minutes surely
mom had never dreamt of being

famous to the world this way
nor when she planned a family thought
she'd be appeasing kids in pain or terror or
in god knows what un-ending rage how can
she possibly contain her other kids, how can they fail
to opportunize on the baby-made commotion sure enough
a wail arises from the middle child a bid for mom's
attention in the fray must she remain
alive for all of them? This baby is

impossibly convulsed, I can't begin to say
how soul-wrenching the screaming is, as if a scalpel were inserted
deep within her ear—who chooses that? Now toddler number three emits
her own exploratory cries but still the nightmare
(having woken up alive) is baby's. All the rest of us
are only irritated, disappointed, lonely, full of words and
wishing to be heard as much
as left alone. Life's awful,

we are slaves, if not
to parents then to poverty
or policy or pain, the grinding at the nerve,
the unexpected growth, or craving, if not
in the others who desire or who despise us, then
in our desiring or despising, under
legacies of time and DNA and
worse: These make us prey

to weepers, leapers, addicts, habits, wedding bells or
verse. Yet given here the chance to fly
for once to someone's aid we all

sat grudgingly and didn't try.

There's Kind, and then There's Kind

My friend felt every carnal suffering and spent
her lifetime nursing damaged animals.
Neurotic parrots liberated from the parrot shop,
the pigeons rescued from the hungers of the hawk,
the dogs delivered to her door—the ones
with chains embedded in their necks
or recoil in their eyes—the ones abandoned
and the ones abused—were given new
protective pens and household latitudes.
Coddled and kibbled, they lost the habit

of their suffering. At large are live
leviathans whose calm
communications can't compare
to our speed-stung technologies. They
were denominated Right because
they floated when harpooned. One

flour beetle, frequently mistaken
for another, got inscribed as The Confused
in taxonomic logs. Another with a hollow in its back
would be remembered as Depressed, by beetle-men.
And once my friend had been informed

her tumors would be terminal,
her husband up and took
a trip, to Paris, with his boyfriend.
There are times that make you want

to burrow deep in some
obliterating bed. But we
leave tracks, or traces, trails.
And much of what we think or say

won't help. He held her later, when a lot
of others were away. What's right? What's
wrong? (What's diagnosable? What's healable?) Today
my friend is dead. But as she had

her last, and worst, and least
time-buying chemo, I remember
what she said: "Now I've felt

everything feelable."

Original

What was the gender
of the foot's original and rightful
owner, so to speak? One wonders

whose foot is it now, if only
legally. A foot alone
washed up. Where is

the rest? All rocks
in this vicinity.
Does this one left

match any of the five
right feet in this coast's
ever-more-macabre panoply?

Is every sixth a part of some
hexameter? How much of every
composition is the silent part. No

question. Not all poetry
is song. Each year the maid
is once again December'd. I would pray

the littlest of
her metatarsals be
hereafter and herewith remembered.

Lament of the Touched
For Ellen, first and last

Detachment's being
thought achievable

is boggling in itself. Its being thought
achievable by love, a love
for all (not only every)
sentience (the human kind and
bestial alike) at times appears

the precept of
intelligences terribly
untouched. How much
of a hand in things must we
promote before

relinquishing the things at hand?
What kiss of mind would such
communal sense permit? A swirl of dust
in schools perhaps . . . Slow learners of
my ilk must spurn

the selving sensualities to feel

for feelers of this kind:
unfasten passion's
burners to discern

whatever's cooler under it.
In short, must court
dispassion just

to *be* compassionate.

Acknowledgments

"The Missing Glove" and "Original": *Free Verse: A Journal of Contemporary Poetry and Poetics*

"The Truly Screaming Baby": *Scoundrel Time*

"Urgent Sickness, Patient Health" is indebted to the author & Niko Boris's translation of "Nurse Sickness, Patient Health" by Blaga Dimitrova in *Because the Sea Is Black* (Wesleyan, 1989).

Thanks to Hugh French of the Tides Institute, Eastport Maine, and to Andrew Steeves of Gaspereau Press in Nova Scotia, for an early broadside of portions of a poem contained here. Thanks also to Adam Ross and the Sewanee Review for their welcoming of more recent work. My poems (like my memories) change shapes and titles, over time, so I may have missed some acknowledgments here. Let me know if so—and I'll sing your praises next time. I've been blessed in kind readers and publishers.

BY RICH HLADKY

Heather McHugh frequents the Salish Sea areas of western Washington State and southern British Columbia. In addition to her 2009 MacArthur Fellowship she has won many distinguished awards for writing and for teaching, having taught for decades at the University of Washington in Seattle, as well as at the MFA Program for Writers at Warren Wilson College (and elsewhere). Between 1979 and 2009 collections of her essays, translations and original poetry regularly appeared in print, but *Feeler* is her first new volume since 2009.

The Quarternote Chapbook Series honors some of the most distinguished poets and prose stylists in contemporary letters and aims to make celebrated writers accesible to all.

Sarabande Books is a nonprofit literary press located in Louisville, KY. Founded in 1994 to champion poetry, short fiction, and essay, we are committed to creating lasting editions that honor exceptional writing. For more information, please visit www.sarabandebooks.org.